COMMUNION

HENRY W. WRIGHT

HENRY W. WRIGHT

Be in Health

4178 Crest Highway
Thomaston, Georgia 30286

www.beinhealth.com

Copyright Notice
© Copyright: 2007 Pleasant Valley Church, Inc.

ISBN 0-9786255-6-0
EAN 978-0-9786255-6-6

All rights reserved. Any material, be it in written form, audio, video, compact disc, website postings – whether it be text, HTML, audio streaming or graphic images related to Pleasant Valley Church, Inc., or Be in Health™ may not be mirrored, reproduced, or displayed in whole or in part on another webpage or website (whatever the nature or purpose), or in any publication or collection of widespread circulation, whether offline or online (whatever the nature or purpose), even if considered "fair use," without express written permission from Be in Health™ or Pleasant Valley Church, Inc.

Disclaimer

This ministry does not seek to be in conflict with any medical or psychiatric practices nor do we seek to be in conflict with any church and its religious doctrines, beliefs or practices. We are not a part of medicine or psychology, yet we work to make them more effective, rather than working against them. We believe many human problems are fundamentally spiritual with associated physiological and psychological manifestations. This information is intended for your general knowledge only. Information is presented only to give insight into disease, its problems and its possible solutions in the area of disease eradication and/or prevention. It is not a substitute for medical advice or treatment for specific medical conditions or disorders. You should seek prompt medical care for any specific health issues. Treatment modalities around your specific health issues are between you and your physician.

As pastors, ministers, and individuals of this ministry, we are not responsible for a person's disease, nor are we responsible for his/her healing. All we can do is share what we see about a problem. We are not professionals; we are not healers. We are only ministers administering the Scriptures, and what they say about this subject, along with what the medical and scientific communities have also observed in line with this insight. There is no guarantee that any person will be healed or any disease be prevented. The fruits of this teaching will come forth out of the relationship between the person and God based on these insights given and applied. This ministry is patterned after the following scriptures: 2 Corinthians 5:18-20; 1 Corinthians 12; Ephesians 4; Mark 16:15-20.

Preface

This booklet was developed from a live teaching to an audience and has been kept in a conversational format. It is designed to reach a personal level with the reader rather than present a structured, theological presentation. Many times the reader will feel that Pastor Henry is talking directly to him or her.

The frequent use of the pronoun *you* is meant to penetrate the human heart for conviction, not for accusation. Pastor Henry has been called to the office of pastor, and as such, he takes care of God's flock.

The purpose of this booklet is to prepare your heart to take communion.

COMMUNION

CONTENTS

A Celebration..1
Love One Another...2
A Way of Life...4
Transition between Covenants....................................5
unleavened bread represented....................................6
Leaven of the Pharisees...6
Leaven in the Body of Christ.......................................7
Never Alone...7
Leaven in a Church...9
Making Peace..13
The Leavened Bread...14
All of the Cup..16
Two Types of Fellowship...18
Highway of Holiness..19
Koinonia..23
The Cup...25
Leavened Church..26
Blessings or Curses...28
Leavened People...30
Communion Means People Together.........................34
Sinners and Communion...35
Grace and Mercy..37
Blocks to Healing...38
Not Discerning the Lord's Body.................................38
The Mystical Body of Christ..39
Denying the Power of the Bread.................................40
Benefits of Communion...41
Strength of Life...45
Instructions for Communion.......................................49
Self-Examination..49

v

Bitterness against Dead People
....**Err**

or! Bookmark not defined.

Angry at God 49
Angry at Yourself 49
One to Another 50
Put the Past in the Past 51
Memory Lane First 52
Misunderstandings 52
Let's pray 53
Instruction in Righteousness 57
The Cup 60
The Bread 61
What <u>Not</u> to Say 61
Lay Down your Life 62
Prayer 62
Safe Place 63
Index 63
Scripture Index 63

COMMUNION

AND THE VERY GOD OF PEACE
SANCTIFY YOU WHOLLY;
AND *I PRAY GOD*
YOUR WHOLE SPIRIT AND SOUL
AND BODY
BE PRESERVED BLAMELESS
UNTO THE COMING
OF OUR LORD JESUS CHRIST.

1 THESSALONIANS 5:23

HENRY W. WRIGHT

COMMUNION
November 2004

As a corporate body, Pleasant Valley Church, like America, is the melting pot of Christianity. People come here from all kinds of backgrounds, persuasions, victories, losses, healthy ways, and bruised ways. God has put us together and expects His kingdom to be formed. As Senior Pastor at Pleasant Valley Church, it has been an interesting journey for me, mixing and matching two kingdoms in each of us: in you, and in me. However, we are all surviving together by the grace of God.

This is an historic time. We have not celebrated communion in this church for quite some time for a number of reasons. The primary reason is that we should not celebrate something we are not living. Many churches celebrate communion as a weekly ritual; others celebrate (observe) it once a month.

A CELEBRATION

Communion is also called the LORD's Supper. Communion is not just celebrating an *historical* event that happened 2,000 years ago. It is celebrating the *living reality* of what happened 2,000 years ago, which is the union of God and man, and man and man, together in *koinonia* fellowship.

LOVE ONE ANOTHER

This union between God and man was made possible by what Jesus accomplished at the cross. The cross represents the vertical relationship between God and man. It also represents the horizontal relationship between each of us in God and in each other.

COMMUNION CELEBRATES RELATIONSHIP: MAN WITH GOD AND MAN WITH MAN

We teach four baptisms at Pleasant Valley Church:

- baptism in water
- baptism with the Holy Ghost
- baptism with fire
- baptism into each other, into the body

(1 Corinthians 12)

Communion represents what Jesus did and the possibility for us to be fully immersed by faith into God and each other. In fact, the Word says you shall know them because of the love they have one for another.

> **By this shall all men know that ye are my disciples, if ye have love one to another.** John 13:35

Sometimes we consider love to be just an absolute covering of sin, without responsibility. Love without responsibility is not scriptural. Love can include reproving as in Proverbs,

COMMUNION

Open rebuke *is* better than secret love.

Proverbs 27:5

Reproving reminded me again of Habakkuk: "What shall I answer the LORD when I am reproved of Him?"

¹I will stand upon my watch, and set me upon the tower, and will watch to see what He will say unto me, and what I shall answer when I am reproved.

²And the LORD answered me, and said, Write the vision, and make *it* plain upon tables, that he may run that readeth it.

³For the vision *is* yet for an appointed time, but at the end it shall speak, and not lie; because it will surely come, it will not tarry.   Habakkuk 2:1-3

The first thing you are told to do, in verse two, is *write the vision*. You write the vision of His will for mankind through the church and through you. Then you *make it plain* on tables and tablets of paper, that he who runs may read the vision. That vision is for an appointed time, and though it seems to tarry as if it would never come, it shall surely come. It will not tarry.

Many people do not want to wait until the reproving time of the LORD is over so that the vision can be executed. Romans says,

...Let every man be fully persuaded in his own mind.   Romans 14:5

3

I promise you, the people of our church here at Pleasant Valley, Donna and I are going to stay and be part of the vision God has given us. We trust God will help us to write the vision He has for us and help us to make it plain so that it would increase.

A WAY OF LIFE

I ask that you open your hearts, because I'm going to read a lot of scripture. I will stop from time to time and make appropriate comments. I remind you today is the 35th day of a 35-day fast in this church.

It seems like yesterday that we decreed a 35-day fast, or a fasted life, concerning who we are, as Pleasant Valley Church.

It was not a fast necessarily for the world or for evangelism. It was a 35-day fast whereby we set ourselves aside before God to prepare our hearts, not just to come and take communion, but *to be prepared to execute it as a way of life*, just as if Jesus were here.

Beginning in Matthew 26:17, you are going to find something very interesting because you are going to read a tradition of the Jews. We will then read the story of the last supper. I was absolutely shocked, when I did a word study on the bread Jesus used.

Transition between Covenants

Sometimes it is amazing what we believe when we have not studied for ourselves. When I began to understand the transition between the Old Covenant and the New Covenant, I also began to understand the transition between the Old Testament Church and the New Testament Church. I began to understand better the types and shadows, and how, in the types and shadows, certain things have been fulfilled and certain things have not been fulfilled.

This instruction will show you a pathway and a journey. Communion is not a happening or a ritual. Communion is a statement of existence, and we will find ourselves caught between an existence which is perfect and that which is imperfect. No one has arrived! There is not one person that is sinless, but you are still being saved by grace. You are still appropriating the works of the cross, by faith, when you appropriate the goodness of God, the Word of God, and the sanctifying work of the Holy Spirit in your lives — day by day, hour by hour, and moment by moment.

As I read, it may seem to be a contradiction until you hear what I have to say. Let's go to Matthew.

> Now the first *day* of the *feast of* the unleavened bread the disciples came to Jesus, saying unto him, Where wilt thou that we prepare for thee to eat the passover? Matthew 26:17

This was a Jewish custom.

UNLEAVENED BREAD REPRESENTED
THE HOLINESS OF GOD

Unfortunately, at the time that Christ came, the Old Testament church, especially the Pharisees, acted and taught as if they were sinless. They celebrated something that they were not. That is a very serious problem to celebrate something that you do not practice or to celebrate something while you point the finger at others saying, "You should be this way", but excuse yourself in it.

> Therefore thou art inexcusable, O man, whosoever thou art that judgest: for wherein thou judgest another, thou condemnest thyself; for thou that judgest doest the same things.   Romans 2:1

This was the condition of the Old Testament church when Jesus came. I want to suggest to you that Jesus came to bridge one covenant to the next. He did not just drop in by parachute. He came, He began to teach, He began to give examples, and He began to demonstrate a new way of thinking, a new way of revelation, and a new way of understanding.

LEAVEN OF THE PHARISEES

To the Pharisees, Jesus was a problem because he exposed the secret thoughts of their heart. The secret thoughts of their heart had not been unleavened. The secret thought of their heart was the leaven He was concerned about. In fact, Jesus warned everyone to beware of the leaven of the Pharisees.

> Then Jesus said unto them, Take heed and beware
> of the leaven of the Pharisees and of the Sadducees.
>
> Matthew 16:6

LEAVEN IN THE BODY OF CHRIST

Even in Christianity today, in certain sectors, we have to be careful that we do not act as if we have no leaven. There is not a person on this earth that does not have some degree of leaven in their life. I say that in order to prepare you to look at something. Let's continue to read.

> [18]And he said, Go into the city to such a man, and say unto him, The Master saith, My time is at hand; I will keep the passover at thy house with my disciples.
> [19]And the disciples did as Jesus had appointed them; and they made ready the passover.
> [20]Now when the even was come, he sat down with the twelve.
>
> Matthew 26:18-20

NEVER ALONE

Communion should never be held between one person and God. I will let you think about that.

You may say, "Well, I'm going to celebrate communion—just me and the LORD. I'm going to get out the bread and the cup, I'm going to sit down at my table and have communion by myself with the LORD."

That is very dangerous, because you cannot have communion with the LORD and leave me out or leave someone else out. It is really interesting that as Jesus began to sit at the last supper, He sat down with those who were close to Him. Do you think His disciples had any leaven? One was a hothead with a revelation. One had a devil. Yes, a member of Jesus' staff had a devil! Oh my! Another one was found to have unbelief and doubt and became known as "Doubting Thomas."

These men were sitting down at Passover indicating that they were supposed to be sinless. Were they sinless? No, not even one was sinless.

We have gathered together corporately. Our Christianity is not an individual thing. You do come before God individually, meet Him by faith and are received of God personally, but you are also part of the corporate body of Christ. The union we call the "body of Christ," is an organism, not an organization, over which He is the head. Jesus said He would keep the Passover with His immediate staff, those who were with Him personally. He sat down with them and then said that one of them would betray Him.

> **20Now when the even was come, he sat down with the twelve.**
> **21And as they did eat, he said, Verily I say unto you, that one of you shall betray me.** Matthew 26:20-21

Betrayal; do you think one of his twelve had leaven? They were exceedingly sorrowful.

> **And they were exceeding sorrowful, and began every one of them to say unto him, Lord, is it I?**
> Matthew 26:22

Is it I that will betray you? Is it me?

COMMUNION

²³And he answered and said, He that dippeth *his* hand with me in the dish, the same shall betray me.

²⁴The Son of man goeth as it is written of him: but woe unto that man by whom the Son of man is betrayed! it had been good for that man if he had not been born.

²⁵Then Judas, which betrayed him, answered and said, Master, is it I? He said unto him, Thou hast said.

Matthew 26:23-25

LEAVEN IN A CHURCH

In the early nineties, I was the pastor of a church in which not everyone loved each other. They came to church together. They sang songs together. They listened to the same sermons. They smiled at each other in passing, but there was this vein of leaven that was not of God. I knew it because it was my job to know it. Of course, that put me on everyone's hit list. Not everyone likes to have government over them.

The government of God has to be compassionate, but sometimes the government of God is very direct and has to establish order and positional things within the kingdom, in love. Otherwise, you have anarchy, chaos, and all kinds of things happen. I knew they were a split church.

I will tell you how bad it was. Prior to this time, I decided to appoint elders in this church. We had been fellowshipping. We were growing. We had 140 people coming every week. It was exciting, and things were happening.

I decided it was time to have the traditional setting of elders and deacons. Rather than make the decision myself, I sent a form to everyone who came to the church. I did not want them to sign it because I did not want to know their identity. I wanted to know who was known in the flock as far as the people were concerned. You know, the people chose Saul because he looked the part. He looked like he would make a good king, but only God knows the secret thoughts of men's hearts.

I prepared them by teaching at least six months about the government of God, and all the things that would be coming. I passed out these forms, and everyone sent them back to me. I went down the list of who the people thought would be a good elder or deacon, and I compiled all the percentages.

I saw those that seemed to stand out as the leaders in my midst, according to the people, and said, "Well, what am I to do with that? Whether I agree or disagree, this is what the people see."

I felt like King David saying, "If you really want me, you are going to have to force me to come back to the throne," because he let the people decide, which was probably wise for him in that particular case.

We had this huge service planned to announce the leaders, and the place was packed out. Then we came to worship, and in the worship, the Spirit of God spoke to me and said, "Can it."

I said, "Do what? Are you the devil talking to me?"

God said, "Do not appoint elders in this church today. Cancel it. Can it. Hold it."

I said, "But LORD, have I been listening to the devil for six months preparing this body to come to this place?"

He said, "No, but I want to teach you something. I want to show you men's hearts like you have never seen them before."

I said, "Yes, sir." So when we came to that place in the service, I stood up and said, "I am sorry, but there will be no appointing of leadership in this church today because God has said, 'Can it!' The appointments are suspended indefinitely. I am sorry. I know you came prepared to hear and to get on with it, but God has said, 'No way. Not today.' "

Well, you could hear a pin drop! Then we finished that service. I do not remember what we talked about, but there were groupings of people who began to surface. At the center of the groupings were several individuals who were drawing people to themselves. The people that were in the center of these circles were not smiling. They were in unhappy circles, and they were the men and the women at the top of the list to be elders and deacons, and they were angry.

I found out later that some of them had their acceptance speeches already planned and typed for reading.

I had gone to no one. I had given no one any indication as to who was even considered. That day, God showed me the subtlety of leaven because each of these individuals had an agenda, and it was not of the kingdom of God. It was their personal agenda. In fact, I told that church about six months later, "This church will not survive, because there is not truly a church here. People in this church have their own agendas."

That church does not exist today, and it should not. So, many times growing up, I learned the hard way about leaven in Christians.

One Sunday morning in that same church, I was there early for the service, knowing the subtlety of the hearts of those that were coming. As people came in the church door, I met them with a cup. It had water in it. As they came through the door, I reached out to them and said, "Would you sup with me?" Everyone would look at me, and look at the cup, and they would withdraw.

You know how it is in a service: some people get there early, some get there on time, and some make it within the hour. As everyone came in, the service did not start, and so people sat there in silence. I waited. Then the next person would come in, just after starting time, and as they would come through the door, I would say, "Good morning. Would you sup from this cup with me?"

They would look at me, and look at the cup, and withdraw. We did that until the last person came through that door. Everyone sat there in silence for almost an hour. I just waited in silence for those who were coming that day.

They were expecting to worship singing, "Praise the LORD" or "I love you God." What they found

12

COMMUNION

was this pastor holding a cup out to them, saying, "Would you take this cup? Would you sup with me?" Not one person in that church touched that cup that day. It was a wise thing for them because of their own leaven.

At the last supper, Jesus was dealing with His own team. Sometimes that is where you have to begin in the kingdom—at home, in your own families, and in your own churches, with your own ministry, and with your own staff members. That is where you find out whether communion is working or not working by what kind of fellowship we have.

MAKING PEACE

Why do you think we have taken 35 days to prepare our hearts for this day?

I have received feedback from many of you, that you privately have been going one to another, and making peace with each other. I am so proud of you. Give yourself a hug because you are preparing to celebrate something that you are living. I said, "Something you are already living." If you intend to celebrate today, and you are not practicing this, then now is your chance to be converted. You are already born again, obviously, but have you been converted since you have been born again?

Repent ye therefore, and be converted, that your sins may be blotted out, when the times of refreshing shall come from the presence of the Lord; Acts 3:19

13

So Jesus is faced with this issue. Jesus is asking the question. He knows that in His own organization there is division, and there is an agenda. There is another kingdom, and He is simply exposing it.

Did Judas repent? Did Judas take that as an occasion to say, "Oh, I am so sorry, LORD? The devil has come into my heart. I do not know where this temptation came from. I cannot stand it! Deliver me, LORD!"

No. Sometimes people are exposed who have leaven in their life. Even if the LORD came to them and pointed His finger at them, and then they said, "I- I- I- I- Is it me, LORD?" Even if He said, "It is as you said," that has not brought them to repentance.

THE LEAVENED BREAD

Now hang on because this is a new revelation for me. I bounced it off Donna, and she told me that those who have traditions of men will come close to stoning me. I was shocked by what I am about to read to you.

> **And as they were eating, Jesus took bread, and blessed** *it*, **and brake** *it*, **and gave** *it* **to the disciples, and said, Take, eat; this is my body.**   Matthew 26:26

I looked up the word "bread" in the Greek. You can do your own word study if you like, and you will be just as shocked as I was. As I was meditating early this morning, the Holy Spirit said, "Henry, look up the word 'bread'."

I said, "Bread?"

"Look up the word 'bread' as it was used in the Greek."

So I looked up the word "bread" in the Greek, and it is *Strong's* Greek #740. It literally says, "A loaf that is raised." It is not unleavened. It was leavened bread that was used at the last supper.

I said, "This cannot be." So I went to the root word, which is *Strong's* Greek #142. It literally says, "to raise." Why, on the Passover, did Jesus use a leavened loaf of bread instead of unleavened like the Pharisees used? He was making a statement that in His midst there was leaven, and He would join Himself to the leaven because He was about to die for the sins of mankind.

Jesus died for a leavened body. This revelation of leavened bread astounded me. I realized we were leaving behind one dispensation of lies for a dispensation of honesty. This would mean we could confess our faults one to another and be healed.

> Confess *your* faults one to another, and pray one for another, that ye may be healed. The effectual fervent prayer of a righteous man availeth much.   James 5:16

Jesus used a loaf of bread that had yeast in it. Read it! I was shocked when I found that Jesus used bread that had risen. You cannot get bread to rise without yeast. I guess that is why Jesus hung out with publicans and sinners. He understood their leaven, and He was saying to His own group with the bread, "You are leavened! One of you has a devil!"

15

They said, "Do *I* have a devil?" I can see Peter, James and John as they said, "Me, LORD? Do *I* have a devil?"

And they were exceeding sorrowful, and began every one of them to say unto him, Lord, is it I?
Matthew 26:22

Judas said, "Do *I* have a devil, LORD? Will *I* betray you?"

Jesus said, "You have said."

Then Judas, which betrayed him, answered and said, Master, is it I? He said unto him, Thou hast said.
Matthew 26:25

Verse 27 says—Drink all of the cup.

And he took the cup, and gave thanks, and gave it to them, saying, Drink ye all of it; Matthew 26:27

ALL OF THE CUP

I wondered what the significance of "all of it" was, and then I realized the shed blood was for forgiveness of *all* sin. When we do not repent for sin as believers, but we have repented for *some* of our sins, we are not drinking *all* of His blood. We are selective in the participation. That is leaven.

WHEN WE REPENT FOR SOME, BUT NOT ALL, OF OUR SINS, THAT IS LEAVEN.

What does the blood represent? Without the shedding of blood, there is no remission of sins. The blood represents remission of sins.

> For this is my blood of the new testament, which is shed for many for the remission of sins.
> Matthew 26:28

> And almost all things are by the law purged with blood; and without shedding of blood is no remission.
> Hebrews 9:22

Continuing in Matthew...

> But I say unto you, I will not drink henceforth of this fruit of the vine ...
> Matthew 26:29

So "fruit of the vine" indicates it was grape juice.

> [29]...until that day when I drink it new with you in my Father's kingdom.
> [30]And when they had sung an hymn, they went out into the mount of Olives.
> Matthew 26:29-30

That is powerful. They sang a song and went to the Mount of Olives.

I want to give you a truth in this conversation of . I do not know if you are prepared to rub shoulders with people that have yucky-puckies. I do not know if you are really prepared to rub shoulders with the world, or if you just want to rain fire down from heaven and kill every one of them.

And when his disciples James and John saw *this*, they said, Lord, wilt thou that we command fire to come down from heaven, and consume them, even as Elias did?
Luke 9:54

Two Types of Fellowship

There are two types of fellowship that Jesus demonstrated. He demonstrated *koinonia* fellowship with those that were His own. He demonstrated He cared, had compassion, and wanted fellowship with those that were the leavened unsaved. Could I say it this way? Jesus demonstrated a compassion for the "leavened saved," and He demonstrated a compassion for the "leavened unsaved."

Jesus demonstrated compassion for the leavened and unleavened.

He could be found with publicans and sinners, caring for their lives. Let's read.

> ³¹Then saith Jesus unto them, All *of* ye shall be offended because of me this night: for it is written, I will smite the shepherd, and the sheep of the flock shall be scattered abroad.
> ³²But after I am risen again, I will go before you into Galilee;
> ³³Peter answered and said unto him, Though all *men* shall be offended because of thee, *yet* will I never be offended.
> ³⁴Jesus said unto him, Verily I say unto thee, That this night, before the cock crow, thou shalt deny me thrice.

COMMUNION

³⁵Peter said unto him, Though I should die with thee, yet will I not deny thee. Likewise also said all the disciples.

³⁶Then cometh Jesus with them unto a place called Gethsemane, and saith unto the disciples, Sit ye here, while I go and pray yonder.

³⁷And he took with him Peter and the two sons of Zebedee, and began to be sorrowful and very heavy.

³⁸Then saith he unto them, My soul is exceeding sorrowful, even unto death: tarry ye here, and watch with me.

³⁹And he went a little further, and fell on his face, and prayed, saying, O my Father, if it be possible, let this cup pass from me: nevertheless not as I will, but as thou wilt.   Matthew 26:31-39

HIGHWAY OF HOLINESS

This brings us to another element of communion. It is not our will; it is the Father's will in our life. It has nothing to do with our will. In fact, our wills probably need to be subjected to the King more than they are today.

Matthew says:

And he cometh unto the disciples, and findeth them asleep, and saith unto Peter, What, could ye not watch with me one hour?   Matthew 26:40

In this discussion today, do not think that I am using this as a method of going black and white with you. We are not black and white; we are all gray. We are coming from point A, and we are going to point Z in this journey called "The Highway of Holiness."

19

We are pilgrims in progress. Our life is a journey and we must understand what the journey consists of. The journey does not involve just going to heaven. It was what Christ did through the cross that made it possible for us to even enter into the journey toward eternity.

This communion service today, on this 35th day of a fasted way of life and thinking, has been designed to help us focus on our journey with God and with each other.

Peter said that he would die for Jesus, yet he could not even stay awake one night. What a guy!

Jesus said,

> 41Watch and pray, that ye enter not into temptation: the spirit indeed *is* willing, but the flesh *is* weak.
> 42He went away again the second time, and prayed, saying, O my Father, if this cup may not pass from me, except I drink it, thy will be done.
> 43And he came and found them asleep again: for their eyes were heavy.
> 44And he left them, and went away again, and prayed the third time, saying the same words.
> 45Then cometh he to his disciples, and saith unto them, Sleep on now, and take *your* rest: behold, the hour is at hand, and the Son of man is betrayed into the hands of sinners.
> 46Rise, let us be going: behold, he is at hand that doth betray me.
> 47And while he yet spake, lo, Judas, one of the twelve, came, and with him a great multitude with swords and staves, from the chief priests and elders of the people.
> 48Now he that betrayed him gave them a sign, saying, Whomsoever I shall kiss, that same is he; hold him fast.   Matthew 26:41-48

We could sit here and talk for hours on the interpersonal relationships of people in churches, or specifically in this body. We pray together. We eat together. We fellowship together. We may even greet each other with a kiss. We may say, "I love you." We may say, "You're my friend." We may say "this" or we may say "that", but all of this is subject to the leaven in us that would interfere.

I think the people in the kingdom of God need to go into a state of continual repenting for not being in that state of being. I think we need to dedicate ourselves to meeting each other, even in our weaknesses, even in our yucky-puckies and even in our idiosyncrasies.

Jesus is bringing this down very clearly in His own life. But He's going to change gears about the outsider. Outsiders are the people not in your circle of fellowship and the people you think are sinners or not sinners.

Going on to verse 49:

49And forthwith he came to Jesus, and said, Hail, master; and kissed him.
50And Jesus said unto him, Friend...Matthew 26:49-50

Oh my! Who did Jesus just call friend? Judas.

50...Friend, wherefore art thou come? Then came they, and laid hands on Jesus, and took him.
51And, behold, one of them which were with Jesus stretched out his hand, and drew his sword, and struck a servant of the high priest, and smote off his ear.

21

> ⁵²Then said Jesus unto him, Put up again thy sword into his place: for all they that take the sword shall perish with the sword.
> ⁵³Thinkest thou that I cannot now pray to my Father, and he shall presently give me more than twelve legions of angels?   Matthew 26:49-53

Jesus is saying (paraphrase), "Do you think your sword would help? I could have called down legions of angels to help Me out of this dilemma."

> ⁵⁴But how then shall the scriptures be fulfilled, that thus it must be?
> ⁵⁵In that same hour said Jesus to the multitudes, Are ye come out as against a thief with swords and staves for to take me? I sat daily with you teaching in the temple, and ye laid no hand on me.
> ⁵⁶But all this was done, that the scriptures of the prophets might be fulfilled...   Matthew 26:54-56

Listen carefully.

> ...Then all the disciples forsook him, and fled.
>   Matthew 26:56

What a team. Jesus lost His entire staff. One of His staff members took a sword and cut off the ear of one of the people with the high priest. Jesus healed that enemy's ear.

FELLOWSHIP INVOLVES
HEALING YOUR ENEMIES

KOINONIA

Sometimes *koinonia* fellowship means being available even for those who don't like you. If we stay around people that are just like us and say good things about us, how much more do the sinners and the publicans do the same with each other?

For if ye love them which love you, what reward have ye? do not even the publicans the same?
Matthew 5:46

We need to extend ourselves. The worst thing that can happen to a body is for cliques to form. Do you know what a clique is? Good buddy groupings. You have the spiritual ones over here, the mid-spiritual ones over there, the learning spiritual ones over here, and the outcasts that need God over there. We make our basis of fellowship around people who agree with us. We make our basis of fellowship around people who do not say the wrong things to us. We make our fellowship around things that are agreeable to us. Are you prepared to make fellowship around things or people that are disagreeable? It's a hard question. Jesus is demonstrating many things in dealing with this subject, and it is all covered in just a few moments of time in this scripture.

Now I want to go to Luke 22 and read it stated somewhat differently.

> ¹⁴And when the hour was come, he sat down, and the twelve apostles with him.
> ¹⁵And he said unto them, With desire I have desired to eat this passover with you before I suffer:
>
> Luke 22:14-15

That fellowship was a decision by Jesus, knowing full well that, according to the prophets, those He was eating with would all leave Him. Would you have the faith for that kind of dinner? Would you sit at the same table, knowing one was going to deny you three times, and one was going to betray you?

I don't know how many times you have sat at table with people who later became enemies to you in the body of Christ. Do not answer too quickly; it has happened to almost everyone here. What are you going to do with that? Are you going to live back there in that place of separation, or are you going to move ahead into what the gospel represents?

Communion represents forgiveness, freedom from the curse, and moving on. Communion is a way of life. It's a state of being. It's a growth pattern. It's something we grow into, but do not get stuck in. When you are out of fellowship, you are stuck in an area where people do not want to be in *koinonia* or fellowship.

So Jesus continues in Luke 22.

> ¹⁶For I say unto you, I will not any more eat thereof, until it be fulfilled in the kingdom of God.
> ¹⁷And he took the cup, and gave thanks, and he said, Take this, and divide *it* among yourselves:
>
> Luke 22:16-17

THE CUP

Now let's talk about the dividing of the cup. We are not going to be using a common cup because of your fears of communicable diseases. There is not enough faith here today to believe that the Spirit of God can kill germs in communion. You know that is true, and the worst thing for you to do is to partake in fear because there is no protection.

So we are going to separate that cup into smaller cups, knowing it came from a common source. We are going to give you individual cups. You must understand what Jesus was doing with the cup when he shared it by giving it to one who would drink, giving it to another who would drink, and then to another who would drink.

The cup and the blood represent the forgiveness of sin, and Jesus was demonstrating that forgiveness is not just between God and you; it also needs to be shared between you and others. Communion is not just a personal deal between God and you.

You may need to repent to God for your breaches with Him. Repent for all your breaches—with God, with others, and with yourself. You may need to repent to each other for your breaches with each other. The same blood that made it possible for you to be forgiven by God for your transgressions and your sins is the same shed blood that makes it possible for you to forgive each other. So this is not just a vertical action; it is vertical <u>and</u> horizontal.

> ¹⁸For I say unto you, I will not drink of the fruit of
> the vine, until the kingdom of God shall come.
> ¹⁹And he took bread... Luke 22:18-19a

I looked up that word "bread" again to make sure it was not another Greek word for "bread", and it's the same word. It means "a loaf." It is impossible to get loaves of bread without yeast. You can get flat bread without yeast. The word "rising" is there in the Greek. I was so shocked to find the word "rising" that I went back to the root word, as I mentioned before. It is just as blunt. Verse 19:

> And he took bread, and gave thanks, and brake it,
> and gave unto them, saying, This is my body which
> is given for you: this do in remembrance of me.
> Luke 22:19

You may say, "Wait a minute. Jesus did not have any sin. Why would He say leavened bread represented His body?"

He may not have had any sin, but the Bible is very clear that He took the sins of all of mankind on Him, and He bore them. He became the sacrificial Lamb. He bore the iniquities and transgressions of many. He took your leaven, so that it would be possible for you to be free.

LEAVENED CHURCH

I do not know if you are ready to accept this, but the Bishop of the Church, the LORD Jesus, is still dealing with a leavened church. We are 2,000 years down the road, and we still are not walking in

COMMUNION

perfection. We still have not mastered repentance from dead works. We have still not mastered faith towards God. We have not mastered the doctrines of baptisms. We have not mastered the laying on of hands. We have not mastered the understanding of the resurrection and eternal judgment.

> ¹Therefore leaving the principles of the doctrine of Christ, let us go on unto perfection; not laying again the foundation of repentance from dead works, and of faith toward God,
> ²Of the doctrine of baptisms, and of laying on of hands, and of resurrection of the dead, and of eternal judgment.   Hebrews 6:1-2

We are just stabbing at something called "Christianity", waiting and begging to go to heaven. Communion does not provide a victory in heaven; it provides a victory here. It represents something that is happening here now. Let's read.

> ²⁰Likewise also the cup after supper, saying, This cup *is* the new testament in my blood, which is shed for you.
> ²¹But, behold, the hand of him that betrayeth me *is* with me on the table.   Luke 22:20-21

Now we have communion between two people who have evil in them. Is that what it says to you? Did Jesus withhold the cup from Judas? Oh my! He did not withhold the cup from Judas. Judas partook of the cup in fraud because he did not have a repentant heart.

We're going to share with you a little bit more in this teaching as to what this means to your life from

27

1 Corinthians 11. Then you will understand why I have not been quick to hold a corporate communion service. I did not want to heap any disease, weakness, and premature deaths on your head. You would have celebrated, but you would not have really understood what it meant for your lives. Most churches that celebrate communion once a week do not totally understand what they are doing; therefore, their churches are filled with disease, psychological problems, weakness, sickness, and even premature death. They celebrate something, but they do not live it. Verse 24, talking about leaven, says there was strife.

And there was also a strife among them, which of them should be accounted the greatest. Luke 22:24

BLESSINGS OR CURSES

I want you to understand that this was happening at dinner, a corporate staff dinner meeting. You always thought the last supper was something that was really wonderful. No. The last supper was either a blessing or judgment, and there was strife between them.

COMMUNION IS EITHER A BLESSING OR A JUDGMENT.

You may not want to hear that. You may not want to receive it, but what you are doing here today is a standard of blessing or curses. You will find your place in it.

If you say, "But I want to keep my leaven and be blessed", then you have not read your Bible recently. You cannot continue to be blessed and continue to be leavened. It is unscriptural. The Christian church is *not* going to be blessed *and* continue serving sin. The Christian church is *not* going to be blessed *and* continue to kill the outsider. The Christian church is *not* going to be blessed *and* continue to have strife, division, competition, and all the rest of it.

Can you imagine? These guys have been with the LORD for about three and a half years, and at dinner they began to have strife about which one of them was the greatest staff member.

"Well, I think I am closer to the LORD than you."

"I think I am really the chosen one."

"So, Judas may have a devil. Did you hear the LORD say Judas was going to betray Him?"

"I don't believe that."

Did Judas believe that?

> 25And he said unto them, The kings of the Gentiles exercise lordship over them; and they that exercise authority upon them are called benefactors.
> 26But ye shall not be so: but he that is greatest among you, let him be as the younger; and he that is chief, as he that doth serve.
> 27For whether is greater, he that sitteth at meat, or he that serveth? *is* not he that sitteth at meat? but I am among you as he that serveth.   Luke 22:25-27

What Jesus said was that the pre-eminence does not go to who sits at dinner together, but to who is your servant. Your greatness is not your position. Your greatness is not who you are as a staff member. Your greatness is not who you are in leadership. Your greatness is, "Are you truly a servant whom the LORD loves?" A lot of people don't really understand "service." Let's go to 1 Corinthians 5:6.

Your glorying is not good. Know ye not that a little leaven leaveneth the whole lump? 1 Corinthians 5:6

LEAVENED PEOPLE

(Pastor is holding a loaf of bread.) This leavened bread today represents us. When you partake of this bread later today, giving a piece to someone else, one to another, what you are really saying to them is, "I have some of this leaven in me, and you have some in you. Can we have our peace together?"

CAN WE HAVE PEACE TOGETHER?

Can we let that which the cross represents mold us and join us together? If this is unleavened bread, then you are signifying that there is no sin in you, and you are a hypocrite. This revelation came into me so strongly. I am teaching you something that is seldom taught. I was astonished at it myself, saying, "God, I am listening to You."

We are so busy looking at each other's leaven that we have missed the good that has been done already. We are busy looking at the areas where our leaven is bumping into someone else's leaven. We have schism

COMMUNION

and division, and we have misunderstood the cross. We have misunderstood the picture. So now we realize we must purge out the old leaven.

Purge out therefore the old leaven...1 Corinthians 5:7

This is instruction for New Testament believers. The Christian church is acting like it does not have a problem. It says, "I am the righteousness of God in Christ Jesus."

> **For he hath made him *to be* sin for us, who knew no sin; that we might be made the righteousness of God in him.** 2 Corinthians 5:21

By faith you are the righteousness of Christ. I said, "*By faith* you are." The church is saying—Behold, all things have passed away. Behold, all things have become new.

> **Therefore if any man *be* in Christ, *he is* a new creature: old things are passed away; behold, all things are become new.** 2 Corinthians 5:17

By faith it is happening that way. Purge out, therefore, the old leaven, that ye may be a new lump. Say with me, "I am a new lump in the making."

You are a new lump, as you are unleavened. Therefore let us keep the feast, not with old leaven, neither with the leaven of malice and wickedness; but with the unleavened bread of sincerity and truth.

> **7Purge out therefore the old leaven, that ye may be a new lump, as ye are unleavened. For even Christ our passover is sacrificed for us:**

31

> **8Therefore let us keep the feast, not with old leaven, neither with the leaven of malice and wickedness; but with the unleavened bread of sincerity and truth.**
> 1 Corinthians 5:7-8

Do you know how to remove the leaven? You just read it. You must begin to take away the things that are the leaven. Then you will not only have the type and shadow of the Passover, you will also have the living proof of the work of the Holy Spirit in your life that is changing you from glory to glory into His image.

> **But we all, with open face beholding as in a glass the glory of the Lord, are changed into the same image from glory to glory, even as by the Spirit of the Lord.**
> 2 Corinthians 3:18

In this communion service, you are telling God and you are telling me as Senior Pastor, that you have made a decision to judge yourself. You have made a decision that you are going to walk in love whether you feel like it or not. You have made a decision that this body is going to represent something that is true instead of something that is fraud.

I hear accusing spirits right now, in the spirit, saying, "Yes, but they just did that to me this morning", or "They said that..." or "They rejected me this morning." That is the leaven. What are you going to do about it? So what if their leaven bumped into you! What are you going to do about it? Are you going to repay leaven with leaven?

COMMUNION

That leaven will leaven the whole lump, and we are not going to have this scripture (that we are being changed from glory to glory) fulfilled, are we?

You may say "Well, I will forgive him when I feel like it."

That is leaven speaking. It has nothing to do with how you feel. Do you think Christ was obedient to the Father because He felt like it? No. He said, "Father, if it be possible, let this cup pass from Me."

> And he went a little further, and fell on his face, and prayed, saying, O my Father, if it be possible, let this cup pass from me: nevertheless not as I will, but as thou wilt. Matthew 26:39

So, it is not going to be convenient to forgive others.

> It is not going to be convenient to love people who have just dumped their leaven on you. However, you are not called to destroy them. You are called to destroy the leaven. How can you destroy the leaven in their life if you have also killed them? So then, what purpose is the cross? You may have a wrong spirit. Do you, eat: this is my body, which is broken for you: this do in remembrance of me.
>
> 25After the same manner also he took the cup, when he had supped, saying, This cup is the new testament in my blood: this do ye, as oft as ye drink it, in remembrance of me. 1 Corinthians 11:24-25

We look back want to call fire down from heaven? Do you want to destroy everyone that has leaven?

33

COMMUNION MEANS PEOPLE TOGETHER

Communion is people together. The LORD was together with His own team. We are not celebrating an historical remembrance. Scripture says, As oft as ye do it, do it in remembrance of Me.

[24]And when he had given thanks, he brake it, and said, Take2,000 years ago, and that is where we leave it. What was said 2,000 years ago needs to be a living reality today. That is why this is called the sacrament of communion.

I have found that there are only three sacraments truly taught in scripture. There may be more, and we can debate about it for days. Foot washing is one of them. The LORD's Supper or communion is another. Water baptism is the third one. Those are essential commandments and critical commandments.

You may say, "Well you have not held a foot washing."

No, I have not held a foot washing. We will do it one day when I think you can bow your knee before someone and really mean it. This is your testing ground, because when you wash someone's feet, you are saying to them, "I accept you with your leaven. How may I serve you? I accept you with your leaven."

What do you think being a pastor is? I am to serve you. I am your brother. I am not your lord. I do not lord over you. In fact, I try to not interfere with your lives. Perhaps I should interrupt your life more often and get in your face more often, with a zeal to propel you into righteousness. But I know you cannot handle it!

Sometimes God uses me to get in people's faces. He is ready to draw a line on the enemy because He is tired of sharing people with devils, and He uses me to get them out. They do one of two things. They either listen to God through me, or they go into rejection and walk out as an enemy (but maybe not forever). Sometimes we do not understand an open rebuke, and sometimes open rebukes have been given with the wrong spirit. This is a long journey in itself.

Open rebuke is better than secret love.
Proverbs 27:5

I want to talk about one of the blocks to healing found in the book, *A More Excellent Way*™. Look at 1 Corinthians 11:27. Of course, back in verses 23 through 26 are the scriptures that we will read later in the actual taking of the cup and the bread, but we cannot read these verses out of context. Many times in Communion services it is out of context, or when it is brought into context, it is used to accuse people and condemn them.

SINNERS AND COMMUNION

I held a communion service in California a few years ago where I invited sinners to come and partake, because I found a scripture in the Old Testament where it was done one time. If that sinner comes and partakes, he is signifying that he

35

understands that Christ died for him, and now a decision has to be made in his life. It calls for a decision. It is a powerful thing that happens when you invite a sinner to communion.

You may say, "Well I do not think you should invite sinners to communion." Then why do we invite sinning saints? Both need to make a decision. If I cannot get a good decision out of a saint, I will take a decision out of a sinner any day. I have to start somewhere.

> 27Wherefore whosoever shall eat this bread, and drink *this* cup of the Lord, unworthily, shall be guilty of the body and the blood of the Lord.
> 28But let a man examine himself, and so let him eat of *that* bread, and drink of *that* cup.
>
> 1 Corinthians 11:27-28

Something called self-examination is involved. We are to examine ourselves for leaven. This scripture is talking about eating and drinking unworthily; you have leaven, but you pretend you don't. I said, "You have leaven, but you pretend you do not have it."

You are aware that the bread we are using for communion has been leavened. This is not unleavened bread, and for me to say this is unleavened bread is fraud.

> 29For he that eateth and drinketh unworthily, eateth and drinketh damnation to himself, not discerning the Lord's body.
> 30For this cause many are weak and sickly among you, and many sleep.
>
> 1 Corinthians 22:29-30

That verse does not mean they sleep in church. It means they die prematurely. I hope you understand Paul is saying that in the corporate body of Christ, many are weak, sick with disease and die prematurely *because* they partake of communion, but do not live it. What you are celebrating in remembrance is that His shed blood is for forgiveness of sins, and His broken body is for the penalty of the curse.

GRACE AND MERCY

Grace was not shed for you. His blood was shed for you. Grace made it possible for His blood to be shed. Grace makes it possible for you to repent and be converted. Grace teaches you what you should know from God. Mercy is a measure of time for you to figure out what He has said for your life.

The blood makes it possible for you to be forgiven. The blood makes it possible for you to be forgiven when you have found yourself serving sin. When you see the leaven in your life, repent to God, and deal with it; then you are forgiven, and you are delivered.

When you are forgiven, His broken body makes it possible for the penalty of serving sin to be broken. Then health and healing should be yours.

Blocks to Healing

Let's talk about three blocks to healing which are critical. I have taught this first block to healing in every Be In Health™ Conference in America.

Not Discerning the Lord's Body

The first block is not discerning the Lord's body. What is meant by "not to discern the Lord's body"?

First of all, the Lord's body means the LORD Himself. It means His shed blood for forgiveness of sin, and His broken body for the penalty of the curse.

You celebrate communion and take the cup, signifying that you understand His shed blood is for forgiveness of sin, but if you have leaven in your life and refuse to acknowledge or repent to God for serving it and allowing it to manifest through you, then for this reason many are sick, weak and die premature deaths.

For this reason many of you are sick and weak and die premature deaths, because you take the cup, but you refuse, as believers, to repent for your participation with sin.

If that is the case, then there is no provision for healing for you because you are not going to get the broken body to work for you *while* you continue in your sins. This is elementary. It's a basic understanding of the righteousness of God through Christ Jesus in our lives.

THE MYSTICAL BODY OF CHRIST

Another aspect of not discerning the LORD's body is that we are the mystical body of Christ. Jesus is the Bishop. He is the Head of the church, the Head of the body. We (each one of us) are the mystical, corporate body of Christ so I am part of you, and you are part of me. The Bible says that God adds to the church daily those that should be saved.

> **Praising God, and having favour with all the people. And the Lord added to the church daily such as should be saved.** Acts 2:47

Then it says that God has placed in the church those, as it has pleased Him.

> **But now hath God set the members every one of them in the body, as it hath pleased him.**
> 1 Corinthians 12:18

So, if you are born again, it means that God has placed you in the body as it has pleased Him, and I am to recognize that you are here because God decided to place you here. I am not to interfere with what God decided, nor am I to injure what God has decided, nor am I to reject what God has decided. I am part of you as a living organism, and you are part of me. If you don't think you are part of me and I am part of you, then you err, and for this reason many of you are weak and sick and die premature deaths.

Even though you may recognize that I am part of you, we end up with an autoimmune disease in the body whereby the body begins to attack the body with debate and strife. We put each other in the stocks and bonds of performance, legalism, control and everything else you can imagine because we begin to eat each other alive. We are filled with envy and jealousy, accusation, bitterness, clamoring and strife; therefore we are diseased.

For this reason many of you are weak, sick and die premature deaths because you celebrate something, but you refuse to be part of it. Now we have the vertical and the horizontal element of the mystical and the actual body of Christ.

DENYING THE POWER OF THE BREAD

The third aspect of communion is to deny the power of what the bread represents. This is a statement I make to churches who have communion every Sunday or once a month. When you say that healing passed away 2,000 years ago with the apostles, you are saying that all we have left from the cross is forgiveness of sin, and the curse is no longer defeated because that, too, passed away with the apostles. When you say that healing is not for today, you are also saying that the curse was not defeated.

In your churches you celebrate communion ritualistically. You *take* the cup and the bread, but you *deny* the bread. So you take the bread but deny the power of what it represents today.

For this reason your churches are filled with people who are sick, diseased, weak and die premature deaths. You deny what you celebrate as part of the sacrament.

I have a word for these denominations that celebrate communion but deny that healing is for today: if you are going to take communion – *do not touch the bread.*

What purpose is it to take the cup if there is no fruit except to go to heaven? What purpose is it to take the cup if you are saying that all God can do today is forgive you of sin? If God cannot be the Great Physician, if He cannot be your Healer, if He cannot be your Deliverer, and if He cannot change your life, then this is heresy at its highest level.

BENEFITS OF COMMUNION

What are the benefits to communion? First of all, the benefit in Matthew 26:28 is forgiveness of sin.

> **For this is my blood of the new testament, which is shed for many for the remission of sins.**
> Matthew 26:28

When we take the cup, we are saying that we are going to repent to God for our sin, and He is going to forgive us. Is that true? No, that is not true.

It is true in part, but let's look at Mark 11:26. If you have an NIV (New International Version) Bible, Mark 11:26 is missing. The NIV has removed a critical scripture that is essential to communion. The King James Version says that if you do not forgive your

41

brother his trespass, neither will your father in heaven forgive you your trespass.

But if ye do not forgive, neither will your Father which is in heaven forgive your trespasses.
Mark 11:26

You cannot call God "Father" unless you are born again. So, this is instruction for those who are born again. It's also found in Matthew 6:14. The NIV translators left it in Matthew 6:14, but they took it out of Mark 11:26.

Listen to me as we as come to communion before the LORD. Maybe you are serving sin, and maybe you have some leaven in your life. We are going to take time for you to privately go before God and repent to Him as your Father. I want Him to forgive you.

It is amazing. We know the LORD's Prayer asks the Father to forgive us our trespasses, as we forgive those who trespass against us.

And forgive us our debts, as we forgive our debtors.
Matthew 6:12

Say this with me. "Forgive us our trespasses, as we forgive those who trespass against us." Listen to what you just said.

FORGIVE US AS WE FORGIVE

Right here you have the condition of forgiveness by God. Church, listen to me.

You are not going to receive from heaven what you will not give away to others

>⁷Blessed *are* the merciful: for they shall obtain mercy.
>⁹Blessed *are* the peacemakers: for they shall be called the children of God. Matthew 5:7,9

You are not going to get from your Father what you will not give to the rest of your Father's kids.

Listen, Church. This is one of the reasons our churches are filled with disease, sickness, and premature death.

It is time to cry out to God. Even when we *see* our yucky puckies, even when we *see* that we are serving sin, even when we *see* the leaven, we say, "Father, I have this in my life, and I repent to you. I hate it and I repent. Will you forgive me for participating with this bitterness?" You cry out to God in repentance at the same time you ask God for favor.

Over here you have six people against whom you are harboring hatred. Over there you have six people with whom you are in strife. Then there is someone else for whom you have resentment and unforgiveness. I am here to tell you with the authority of the Word of God, with the words of Jesus Himself, that if you stand praying, and you ask God to forgive you, yet you will not forgive everyone, living or dead, of their trespass, then you are wasting your time if you are believers.

You may say, "I don't like that."

Do not take it up with me; take it up with the Boss (God). He is the one who wrote this. For those who have taken Mark 11:26 out of the Bible, woe unto you that you would try to give God's people false security.

> **And if any man shall take away from the words of the book of this prophecy, God shall take away his part out of the book of life, and out of the holy city, and *from* the things which are written in this book.**
> Revelation 22:19

No wonder your churches are filled with disease and sickness and premature death, because you fraudulently celebrate something you refuse to do.

We at Pleasant Valley are just now forming into a body that really begins to understand communion. You have weathered the test. Your hearts have been tried by ungodly men who have come and gone. Your hearts have been tried, and you have been sifted. You have been tried, and maybe you are still being tried, but you have been found faithful. As the senior pastor of this church, I call you faithful and welcome you to the communion of the saints.

It does not mean that when you come to the communion of the saints, you do not still have some of this in you, but it tells me you understand. It tells me you have a hatred for leaven, and it tells me you are about to bear each other's burdens and not kill each other in the future. That makes me a happy pastor. Psalm 103 tells us the LORD forgives us of all of our transgressions, and He heals us of all of our diseases.

COMMUNION

Who forgiveth all thine inquities; who healeth all thy diseases. Psalm 103:3

Maybe we have had transgressions and did not recognize them. Maybe we have had leaven and did not recognize it. Sometimes we are in denial. Sometimes we just do not see it. Sometimes we have become so one with sin that we are not even able to separate our own personalities from it, and we serve it as if it were our own psychology.

STRENGTH OF LIFE

First Corinthians offers something else in forgiveness and walking in love: Strength of life, not dying prematurely, and no sickness or disease. Not getting sick and walking in divine health is better than healing.

> [29]**For he that eateth and drinketh unworthily, eateth and drinketh damnation to himself, not discerning the Lord's body.**
> [30]**For this cause many** *are* **weak and sickly among you, and many sleep.**
> [31]**For if we would judge ourselves, we should not be judged.** 1 Corinthians 11:29-31

If you understand this teaching, what is happening today totally represents good things for your life; however, we are not going to have good things for our life when we continue to allow leaven to rule unhindered and unchecked.

Let's turn to 1 Peter 2 and read the entire chapter.

45

¹Wherefore laying aside all malice, and all guile, and hypocrisies, and envies, and all evil speakings,

²As newborn babes, desire the sincere milk of the word, that ye may grow thereby:

³If so be ye have tasted that the Lord *is* gracious.

⁴To whom coming, *as unto* a living stone, disallowed indeed of men, but chosen of God, *and* precious,

⁵Ye also, as lively stones, are built up a spiritual house, an holy priesthood, to offer up spiritual sacrifices, acceptable to God by Jesus Christ.

⁶Wherefore also it is contained in the scripture, Behold, I lay in Sion a chief corner stone, elect, precious: and he that believeth on him shall not be confounded.

⁷Unto you therefore which believe *he is* precious: but unto them which be disobedient, the stone which the builders disallowed, the same is made the head of the corner,

⁸And a stone of stumbling, and a rock of offence, *even to them* which stumble at the word, being disobedient: whereunto also they were appointed.

⁹But ye *are* a chosen generation, a royal priesthood, an holy nation, a peculiar people; that ye should shew forth the praises of him who hath called you out of darkness into his marvellous light:

¹⁰Which in time past *were* not a people, but *are* now the people of God: which had not obtained mercy, but now have obtained mercy.

¹¹Dearly beloved, I beseech *you* as strangers and pilgrims, abstain from fleshly lusts, which war against the soul;

¹²Having your conversation honest among the Gentiles: that, whereas they speak against you as evildoers, they may by *your* good works, which they shall behold glorify God in the day of visitation.

¹³Submit yourselves to every ordinance of man for the Lord's sake: whether it be to the king, as supreme;

COMMUNION

¹⁴Or unto governors, as unto them that are sent by him for the punishment of evildoers, and for the praise of them that do well.

¹⁵For so is the will of God, that with well doing ye may put to silence the ignorance of foolish men:

¹⁶As free, and not using *your* liberty for a cloak of maliciousness, but as the servants of God.

¹⁷Honour all *men*. Love the brotherhood. Fear God. Honour the king.

¹⁸Servants, *be* subject to *your* masters with all fear; not only to the good and gentle, but also to the froward.

¹⁹For this *is* thankworthy, if a man for conscience toward God endure grief, suffering wrongfully.

²⁰For what glory *is it*, if, when ye be buffeted for your faults, ye shall take it patiently? but if, when ye do well, and suffer *for it*, ye take it patiently, this *is* acceptable with God.

²¹For even hereunto were ye called: because Christ also suffered for us, leaving us as an example, that ye should follow his steps:

²²Who did no sin, neither was guile found in his mouth: ²³Who, when he was reviled, reviled not again; when he suffered, he threatened not; but committed *himself* to him that judgeth righteously:

²⁴Who his own self bare our sins in his own body on the tree, that we, being dead to sins, should live unto righteousness: by whose stripes ye were healed.

²⁵For ye were as sheep going astray; but are now returned unto the Shepherd and Bishop of your souls.   1 Peter 2:1-25

That is a powerful chapter for this communion day and for this time of reflection in our lives.

So now, I want to take you to some rejoicing. I want to show you some happiness and show you the pathway. I want to show you the fruit of what communion represents. I want to take you to Isaiah 35

47

and read the entire chapter to you. Just listen to it, and then we will move into a song.

¹The wilderness and the solitary place shall be glad for them; and the desert shall rejoice, and blossom as the rose.

²It shall blossom abundantly, and rejoice even with joy and singing: the glory of Lebanon shall be given unto it, the excellency of Carmel and Sharon, they shall see the glory of the Lord, and the excellency of our God.

³Strengthen ye the weak hands, and confirm the feeble knees.

⁴Say to them *that are* of a fearful heart, Be strong, fear not: behold, your God will come *with* vengeance, even God *with* a recompence; he will come and save you.

⁵Then the eyes of the blind shall be opened, and the ears of the deaf shall be unstopped.

⁶Then shall the lame *man* leap as an hart, and the tongue of the dumb sing: for in the wilderness shall waters break out, and streams in the desert.

⁷And the parched ground shall become a pool, and the thirsty land springs of water: in the habitation of dragons, where each lay, shall be grass with reeds and rushes.

⁸And an highway *shall be* there, and a way, and it shall be called The way of holiness; the unclean shall not pass over it; but it *shall be* for those: the wayfaring men, though fools, shall not err *therein*.

⁹No lion shall be there, nor *any* ravenous beast shall go up thereon, it shall not be found there; but the redeemed shall walk *there*:

¹⁰And the ransomed of the Lord shall return, and come to Zion with songs and everlasting joy upon their heads: they shall obtain joy and gladness, and sorrow and sighing shall flee away.   Isaiah 35:1-10

God bless you!

INSTRUCTIONS FOR COMMUNION

SELF-EXAMINATION

Let's go to 1 Corinthians chapter 11 again. Then I want to privately take some time before the LORD. In this time of private reflection, personally before God, I want you to prepare to forgive everyone, living or dead.

BITTERNESS AGAINST DEAD PEOPLE

I have met quite a few people over the years that still have bitterness against dead people. It is just not worth it to be diseased because of someone who is dead.

ANGRY AT GOD

Maybe some of you have bitterness against God. You have had a battle with religious spirits that have accused God. Maybe some of you did not see the connection between sin and disease, and you have blamed God for your diseases.

ANGRY AT YOURSELF

Maybe you have bitterness or unforgiveness against yourself. Some of you have shame and guilt from past sins that you have repented for, but you still will not release yourself because accusing spirits continue to accuse you to yourself and make you feel unclean, ungodly and unworthy.

49

In this time of reflection, I want to give you a chance to sincerely do that. God hears you. He not only hears you, He knows the thoughts of your heart.

I want to talk to our Father in prayer in just a moment. Then I want some of the men to come up here and first offer the cup, and then the bread.

ONE TO ANOTHER

We want everyone to have a piece of bread and go one to another, to everyone that is here, from the youngest to the oldest as you so desire.

If you are here this morning, and you do not want to partake of this communion, no one is going to make you, and no one is going to look down at you because you do not partake. This is done out of your own heart so there is no stigma if you do not participate.

I am going to tell you what "one to another" means, and we are not leaving this building until it is finished. We are going to go one to another until "everyone has gone to everyone." You might miss one or two because of the logistics of how many people are here, but it will not be done because you have an evil heart. Do not go into guilt and condemnation, thinking God is mad at you because you missed nine people, but do not deliberately avoid anyone.

When you go to a person, take a piece of this bread and give it to them. Do not take big pieces because we are not going to gorge on this, and do not be worried about what falls on the floor. French bread is just too crusty and crumbly so we have used Italian bread. Please try not to spill the cup because we are not ready to put down new carpet.

PUT THE PAST IN THE PAST

There may be some in here who in the past have celebrated communion from a ritualistic, religious standpoint. Maybe you were not taught what it really represented. Maybe you thought it was just remembering that Jesus died for you and that you said yes to Him. That is a historical thing. "I thank You, LORD, for dying for me." But, you did not recognize what the cross represents in everyday life and everyday being.

If you have celebrated communion unworthily in the past, just tell God you did not understand. In your private prayer time, say, "God, I was not taught. I just did not understand. I am sorry." Repent and say, "God, thank You for teaching me. I understand this now." You know what He is going to do? Forgive you.

WILL YOU FORGIVE YOURSELF?
WILL YOU FORGIVE OTHERS?

MEMORY LANE FIRST

There is one thing I want you to do here before you go to others. I want you to allow the Holy Spirit to take you on a journey. When we have this silent time, we are going to take four or five minutes for each of you, personally and individually to allow the Holy Spirit to take you to memory lane.

I am not into visualization, but you know who you have bitterness against. You know who has hurt you. Do not give me an intellectual or over-spiritual, "Aaah, I forgive them." When you think about their name and their face, and feel something in the pit of your stomach, that is bitterness, and you need to get rid of it.

So I want you to take your time before God; then we will go one to another in communion. Finally we will come back together even if we are not totally finished. At some point we will just bring you back together. Some of you may have some serious talking to do. I have heard that some of you have already done your serious talking between each other before this service.

MISUNDERSTANDINGS

I do not care if we agree or disagree. There can be no schism between us. Those disagreements that we have are usually because of ignorance anyway. It is usually because of misunderstandings.

Do you know the reason for misunderstandings? God gave me that revelation many years ago. It is a

COMMUNION

powerful revelation of the root behind misunderstandings. The root behind all misunderstandings is just that someone did not understand. Someone just did not have the facts. We have developed wars, clashes, and separations over ignorance and misunderstanding.

LET'S PRAY

Father, I do not take this lightly. I myself am one of these people. I am just a man. I have my leaven. They have their leaven, but You decided to be in fellowship with those who had sin, whether they were chosen or they were Gentile. You loved them so You offered Your fellowship.

LORD, the way You think is how the Father thinks. The way You acted and how You thought is really what God the Father wanted You to do and say. So we see that is what the Father wants us to do. LORD Jesus, You made it possible for us to understand this and be able to execute it.

Father, I know You are looking down at this congregation, this body of believers. There are people like us, Father, all over the world, having communion the way they see it and the way they understand it. I know, Father, You are bigger and greater than even what we are doing. We probably do not even see it clearly yet, but we see enough of it that we are doing it this way. We feel that it is scriptural, and we think that it would be Your heart today.

53

So, Father, in this time I ask that You, by the Spirit of God in the name of Jesus, would open the hearts of these people. These are a precious people. There is not one person in this room, Father, that is inferior or insignificant or greater than another. One has been given one gift. One has been given five. One has been given ten.

When we begin to compare ourselves to the burden of the people You may have placed on one or another, to a greater measure because of the ability to serve You a little more, it does not make us greater than the other. Every part of the body supplies the effectual measure of building up to that part of the body. We need each other so desperately, and there are things in these people that I need, God. There are things in me that they need. Together we have needs from each other, and sin tries to keep it from coming to a place of fruition.

We acknowledge before You, God, in this ceremony, that as this leavened bread is here, we are also a leavened people. We also understand that by Your cross we have the ability to appropriate, by faith and obedience, the good things of heaven, and that we may be changed and grow up in all things into You. We are going to put away foolish things to the best of our ability. We are going to walk in love and forgiveness to the best of our ability so that He who was sinless may perfect us.

Heavenly Father, the Father of all spirits, thank You for creating us through Jesus Christ, and saving us through Jesus Christ. Father God in heaven, I know You are watching this service. Thank You for making it possible, and LORD Jesus, thank You for making it possible. Holy Spirit, thank You for coming and being obedient to the will and the Word of the living God for us. We are just people, God; we are just dust.

Father, I ask You to soften hearts here today. God, I ask You to release Your Spirit to bring tenderness of heart and softness of heart. Let this not be like a New Year's resolution that fades by tomorrow morning. Let this service today be an historic and never-ending movement of Your Spirit and Your power, and Your love, and Your personage in this people. I cannot speak for the rest of the churches in America. I cannot speak for the rest of the people. I cannot speak for anyone else. You have put me in this sheepfold, and I take responsibility for it before You.

Give me the wisdom, Father, and those that are here serving with me, to bring this flock into green pastures, to bring this flock into a place that it is at peace with You and with each other. Let the world look in at some point and say, "Yes, God is in their midst," because nothing happens apart from You, God. So Father, by Your Spirit, I release Your will, Your ways, Your Word, and Your heart, into this Your people in the name of Jesus. Amen.

We will go through the scriptures, and then we will take the cup first. I am reading 1 Corinthians chapter 11.

²³For I have received of the Lord that which also I delivered unto you, That the Lord Jesus the *same* night in which he was betrayed took bread:

²⁴And when he had given thanks, he brake *it,* and said, Take, eat: this is my body, which is broken for you: this do in remembrance of me.

²⁵And after the same manner also *he took* the cup, when he had supped, saying, This cup is the new testament in my blood: this do ye, as oft as ye drink *it,* in remembrance of me.

²⁶For as often as ye eat this bread, and drink this cup, ye do shew the Lord's death till he come.

²⁷Wherefore whosoever shall eat this bread, and drink *thi*s cup of the Lord, unworthily, shall be guilty of the body and blood of the Lord.

²⁸But let a man examine himself, and so let him eat of *that* bread, and drink of that cup.

²⁹For he that eateth and drinketh unworthily, eateth and drinketh damnation to himself, not discerning the Lord's body.

³⁰For this cause many *are* weak and sickly among you, and many sleep.

³¹For if we would judge ourselves, we should not be judged.

³²But when we are judged, we are chastened of the Lord, that we should not be condemned with the world.

³³Wherefore, my brethren, when ye come together to eat, tarry one for another.

³⁴And if any man hunger, let him eat at home; that ye come not together unto condemnation. And the rest will I set in order when I come.

1 Corinthians 11:23-34

INSTRUCTION IN RIGHTEOUSNESS

This is instruction in righteousness for the church. Let's take four or five minutes and hold a time of reflection. Take this time to privately and quietly make our peace with God, about ourselves, and others.

Just let it go, people, whatever it is. Do not hang on to anything. It is not worth it. It does not mean that because you are here, all your leaven will leave, but it prepares the way for God to deal with you and to remove it.

The first thing that must happen with God is decision. There has to be a decision made. Make a choice. Choose this day what you will have - life or death, blessings or cursings.

> I call heaven and earth to record this day against you, *that* I have set before you life and death, blessing and cursing: therefore choose life, that both thou and thy seed may live: Deuteronomy 30:19

It is your life. He gave it to you. Pick it back up, not in guilt, not in condemnation, but in faith. If you have some leaven in your life, tell it, "I am not going to drag you along with me until you are gone. I am going to deal with you." Begin to confront it in your life. Talk to it. Say, "No way."

You may say, "Talk to leaven?"

Sure. It is talking to you.

Father, I thank You for being here this morning to deal with our hearts. Thank You, Father!

I did hear something in my spirit saying that some of you do not know how to approach God. Maybe some of you are still afraid of Him. Some of you are still hiding in religion. You are hiding in your fears.

If the Spirit of God would speak through me right now, I have something to say to you. The Holy Spirit is reminding me of a scripture that I read to you already, that if Jesus called Judas "friend" in the betrayal, how much more is He calling you friends? Jesus said, I no longer call you servants, but I call you friends.

> **Henceforth I call you not servants; for the servant knoweth not what his lord doeth: but I have called you friends; for all things that I have heard of my Father I have made known unto you.** John 15:15

I met an enemy recently. Well, they are not an enemy, but there have been difficulties. I met them, and I had not seen them in a long time. I remember giving them a hug and, the first thing I said was so amazing. I said, "Hello, friend." You know, that is who we are. Whether we have iniquity between us and God, whether we have leaven between each other, we are friends.

Have you prepared to be a friend to someone next to you?

You may say, "I don't even like them."

I understand totally how you feel. If Jesus called us friends, then is Jesus our friend? Are we a friend of Jesus? Wait a minute. If Jesus is your friend and my friend, if you are Jesus' friend, and I am Jesus' friend, then who has to be friends? We are going to have to be friends with each other because we are mutual friends of Jesus.

I do not think we really understand friendship like we need to. Sometimes friendship is, "What can you do for me?" True friendship is, "How can I serve you?" True friendship is, "I do not need anything from you." True friendship is not based on what you can give or receive. True friendship is just people that like being together.

There is always something in each of your lives so that you can find common ground.

Gentlemen, take the trays and go into the audience, and make sure that everyone has a cup, young and old, children included. Those of you who have real young children are going to have to hold their cup for them. I want our children to experience this even though some of them may not be at the years of understanding.

We are not saying that they are being sanctified by the cup. We are saying that we are teaching right now, even our families, to experience the way they should go. Teach a child the way he should go, and when he is old, he shall not depart from it. I wish it said "older" instead of "old."

Train up a child in the way he should go: and when he is old, he will not depart from it. Proverbs 22:6

THE CUP

This cup signifies that we now have access to our Father in heaven through Jesus Christ. No greater love is there than a man who would lay his life down for another.

> **Greater love hath no man than this, that a man lay down his life for his friends.**　　　John 15:13

This cup signifies that Jesus died that we may live. Even as you are being forgiven, so forgive others. Every person in this room has something within you that will offend someone else at some point. We have expectations. We have needs. We have need of approval. We have need of acceptance. We have a need of a state of being or belonging. That leaven within us sometimes reaches out incorrectly for acceptance or approval. I promise you no one here is going to do the right thing all the time, so you might as well just get used to it. What we do after the fact is the litmus test.

After this manner also he took the cup.

> **After the same manner also *he took* the cup, when he had supped, saying, This cup is the new testament in my blood: this do ye, as oft as ye drink it, in remembrance of me.**　　　1 Corinthians 11:25

You may take the cup.

Thank You, Father. Thank You, LORD Jesus. You loved us so much. You endured the pain, the suffering as a human that we may live. Let your life live through us. Give us hearts to forgive others all

COMMUNION

the time, whether we feel like it or not. For as we are forgiven, so we forgive others. As we forgive others their trespasses, we are forgiven. Thank You, Father.

Let's gather the cups. Just turn them in and we will stack them.

THE BREAD

Gentlemen, I want you to spread out. Go to a couple of rows and break the bread in big chunks. In your rows, just break it up among each other until everyone has a big chunk. As you give other people pieces of bread, they are going to give you some. Just take little bites because we want to eat dinner later.

I am going to read some more scriptures, and then we are going to begin. When you go one to another, you do not have to get involved in a long dissertation of past wrongs.

WHAT NOT TO SAY

Here is what you should not do, "Well I forgive you for hating me" or "I forgive you for rejecting me." Please do not do this! It is because bitterness is speaking. Please say instead, "I have had bitterness" or "I have had misunderstandings."

Most of you, when you come to each other, just need to say, "I love you." Give each other a hug. Give each other a little piece of bread.

> [23]For I have received of the Lord that which I also delivered unto you, That the Lord Jesus the *same* night in which he was betrayed took bread:

61

²⁴**And when he had given thanks, he brake** *it*, **and said, Take, eat: this is my body, which is broken for you: this do in remembrance of me.**

1 Corinthians 11:23-24

LAY DOWN YOUR LIFE

I do not know if you all understand the concept of being broken for each other. It is one thing to forgive each other, but are you truly ready to lay your life down for someone else? No greater love is there than a man who would lay his life down for another. That is love. He that would be greatest amongst you would be the greatest servant.

But he that is greatest among you shall be your servant. Matthew 23:11

You may take the Bread.

PRAYER

Father, I thank You for this time as we go one to another. Maybe there are people who do not even know each other. Maybe you have only seen them in church. Well, they are part of Your body. You might bump into the intestine, and not even know it. (You bumped into the intestine a long time ago because I am the intestine. I help you process food and get rid of waste.)

Father, as we go one to another, work with us. If anything gets stirred up within us or if we have buried anything between each other, Father, let it not be a festering sore, but a healing wound this day, in the name of Jesus. Amen.

... TIME OF COMMUNION TAKES PLACE ...

I hope we take this spirit of fellowship, this communion of the saints, and the great God who made it possible, not as a happening, but as an ember that glows. I trust the Holy Spirit to fan us and make us one. We may have to work through some leaven. We may have to work through some yucky-puckies, but you cannot go anywhere if you do not know where you are going. We know where we are going.

SAFE PLACE

As a pastor, I honor all of you here today. I honor you for the integrity of your decision. I honor you for your big hearts. I know God your Father is happy and pleased to see you mingling one with another. He will release the Spirit of God to continue what He has started. Anything that would interfere with the Spirit of God and the peace of God has to go. I know our pastors and leaders all commit to making Pleasant Valley Church a safe place for all men. The seed of it will go around the world so that the kingdom of God can be a safe place for those who find it.

I am pleased today, even in just making the contact with each other, I am pleased. We truly do not take enough time for each other. We are so busy with life and things, and sometimes we get trapped in isolation. I encourage all of you to reach out to others you do not even know. We have so many new people coming here.

I want to encourage you all to get to know each other. Drop in by phone (not to gossip, not to leaven anything), but let's begin to exhort each other. Call someone and say, "I am not trying to make anything happen. I just want to exhort you and build you up. I want to read you a couple of verses from the Bible."

Do not use it for a dumping ground or for a long hour of "Let me tell you about my problems." Use it for a time of connection, and of fellowship. "Can I pray for you?" You can be on the phone and gone in five minutes.

I know God will begin to work with us. Some of you are desperately lonely, and some of you are afraid. That is the leaven of fear that you are still struggling with as to whether people love you or do not love you, and whether you can accept their love or not. I want to encourage you to bust out of your prison houses! Bust out, and come into the body. Be part of the body. I just want to encourage you in that today. Let's meditate on the things that you have heard from the Word today. Let's mediate on what communion truly means. Let God be our Father, and Jesus be our LORD, and let's release the Holy Spirit to get it all done, in the name of Jesus. Amen.

INDEX

Accusing.............. 32, 49

Appropriate 4, 5, 54

Baptisms 2, 27

Betray............8, 9, 16, 20, 24, 29

Bitterness 40, 43, 49, 52, 61

Blessing................ 28, 57

Block..................... 38, 51

Blood............. 16, 17, 25, 27, 33, 36, 37, 38, 41, 56, 60

Body 1, 2, 8, 11, 14, 15, 21, 23, 24, 26, 32, 33, 36, 37, 38, 39, 40, 44, 45, 47, 53, 54, 56, 62, 64

Bread.............4, 5, 6, 7, 14, 15, 26, 30, 31, 32, 35, 36, 40, 41, 50, 51, 54, 56, 61

Broken...........33, 37, 38, 56, 62

Celebrate.......1, 6, 7, 13, 28, 38, 40, 41, 44

Cliques 23

Compassion 18

Corporate......1, 8, 28, 37, 39

Covenant 6

Cup................7, 12, 13, 16, 19, 20, 24, 25, 27, 33, 35, 36, 38, 40, 41, 50, 51, 56, 59, 60

Curses 28

Dead works 27

Deny........ 18, 19, 24, 40, 41

Die15, 19, 20, 37, 38, 39, 40

Dispensation 15

Division 14, 29, 31

Fellowship..........1, 13, 18, 21, 23, 24, 53, 63, 64

Forgiveness 16, 24, 25, 37, 38, 40, 41, 42, 45, 54

Freedom.................... 24

Friend.................. 21, 58

Government.......... 9, 10

Grace 1, 5

Holiness................ 6, 48

Horizontal 2, 25, 40

65

Instruction..........5, 31, 42, 57

Judgment............. 27, 28

Koinonia 1, 18, 23, 24

Lamb 26

Leadership........... 11, 30

Leaven..............6, 7, 8, 9, 11, 12, 13, 14, 15, 16, 17, 21, 26, 28, 29, 30, 31, 32, 33, 34, 36, 37, 38, 42, 43, 44, 45, 53, 57, 58, 60, 63, 64

Misunderstanding.... 53

Mystical 39, 40

Organism............... 8, 39

Passover........... 8, 15, 32

Pilgrim 20, 46

Purge........................... 31

Rebuke 3, 35

Relationship 2

Repent..............14, 16, 17, 25, 37, 38, 41, 42, 43

Righteousness31, 35, 38, 47, 57

Sacrament............ 34, 41

Self-examination....... 36

Servant.............21, 30, 58, 62

Serve.................29, 34, 45, 54, 59

Sinless 5, 6, 8, 54

Sinner 35, 36

Strife 28, 29, 40, 43

Thanks 16, 24, 26, 34, 56, 62

Together...........1, 8, 9, 21, 29, 30, 34, 52, 56, 59

Type and shadow..... 32

Scripture Index

Psalm 103:3 45

Proverbs 22:6 59

Proverbs 27:5 .... 3, 35

Isaiah 35:1-10 48

Habakkuk 2:1-3 3

Matthew 5:7,9 43

Matthew 5:46 23

Matthew 6:12 42

Matthew 16:6 7

Matthew 23:11 62

Matthew 26:17 .... 4, 5

Matthew 26:20 8

Matthew 26:20-21 8

Matthew 26:22 ..... 8, 16

Matthew 26:23-25 9

Matthew 26:25 16

Matthew 26:26 14

Matthew 26:28 ... 17, 41

Matthew 26:29 17

Matthew 26:29-30.... 17

Matthew 26:31-39.... 19

Matthew 26:39 33

Matthew 26:40 19

Matthew 26:41-48.... 20

Matthew 26:49-50.... 21

Matthew 26:49-53.... 22

Matthew 26:56 22

Mark 11:26.... 41, 42, 44

Luke 22:14-15 24

Luke 22:16-17 24

Luke 22:18-19 26

Luke 22:19 26

Luke 22:20-21 27

Luke 22:24 28

Luke 22:25-27 29

John 13:35 2

John 15:13 60

Acts 2:47 39

Acts 3:19 13

Romans 2:1 6

Romans 14:5 3

1 Corinthians 5:6 30

1 Corinthians 5:7....
.... 31, 32

1 Corinthians 5:7-8 .. 32

1 Corinthians 11:23-24 62

1 Corinthians 11:24-25 33

1 Corinthians 11:25 60

1 Corinthians 11:27-28 36

1 Corinthians 11:29-31 45

1 Corinthians 12:18 39

1 Corinthians 22:29-30 36

2 Corinthians 3:18 32

2 Corinthians 5:17 31

2 Corinthians 5:21 31

Hebrews 6:1-2 27

Hebrews 9:22 17

James 5:16 15

1 Peter 2:1-25 47